The World of Composers

Chopin

Greta Cencetti

PETER BEDRICK BOOKS

McGraw-Hill
Children's Publishing
A Division of The McGraw·Hill Companies

This edition published in the United States in 2002 by
Peter Bedrick Books, an imprint of
McGraw-Hill Children's Publishing,
A Division of The McGraw-Hill Companies
8787 Orion Place
Columbus, Ohio 43240

www.MHkids.com

ISBN 1-58845-469-X

Library of Congress Cataloging-in-Publication Data

Cencetti, Greta.
Chopin / Greta Cencetti.
p. cm. -- (The world of composers)
Summary: An introduction to the life and musical career
of the nineteenth-century Polish pianist and composer.
ISBN 1-58845-469-X
1. Chopin, Frederic, 1810-1849--Juvenile literature. 2. Composers—Biography—
Juvenile literature. [1. Chopin, Frederic, 1810-1849.
2. Composers.] I. Title. II. Series.

ML3930.C46 C46 2002
786.2'092--dc21
[B]
2001052559

© 2002 Ta Chien Publishing Co., Ltd.
© 2002 Studio Mouse

10 9 8 7 6 5 4 3 2 1 CHRT 06 05 04 03 02

Printed in China.

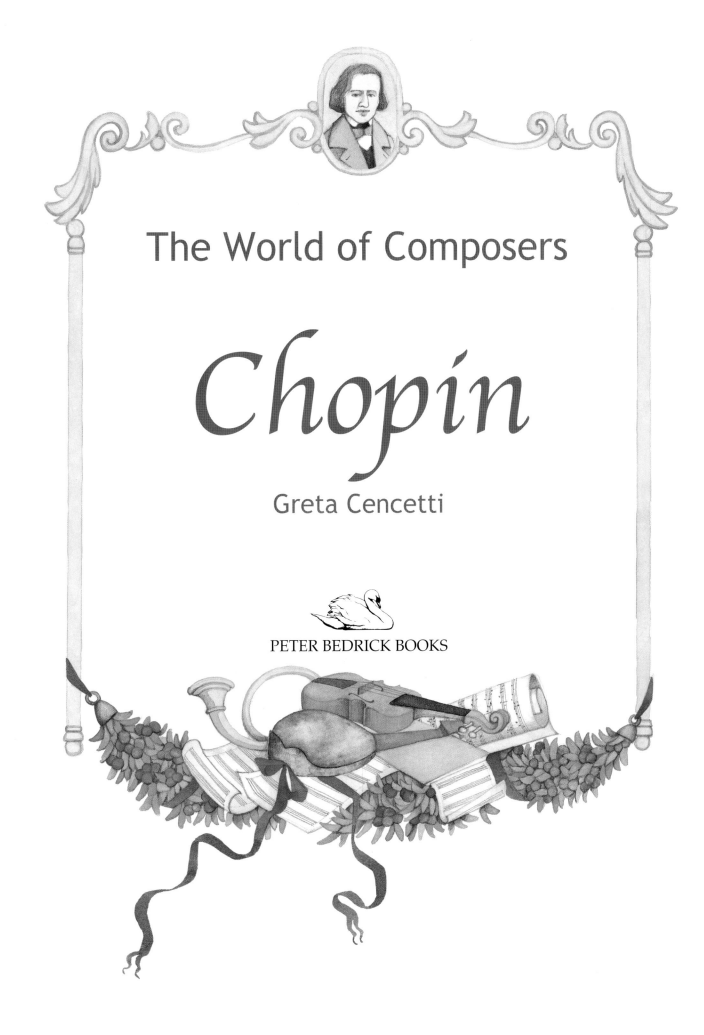

The World of Composers

Chopin

Greta Cencetti

PETER BEDRICK BOOKS

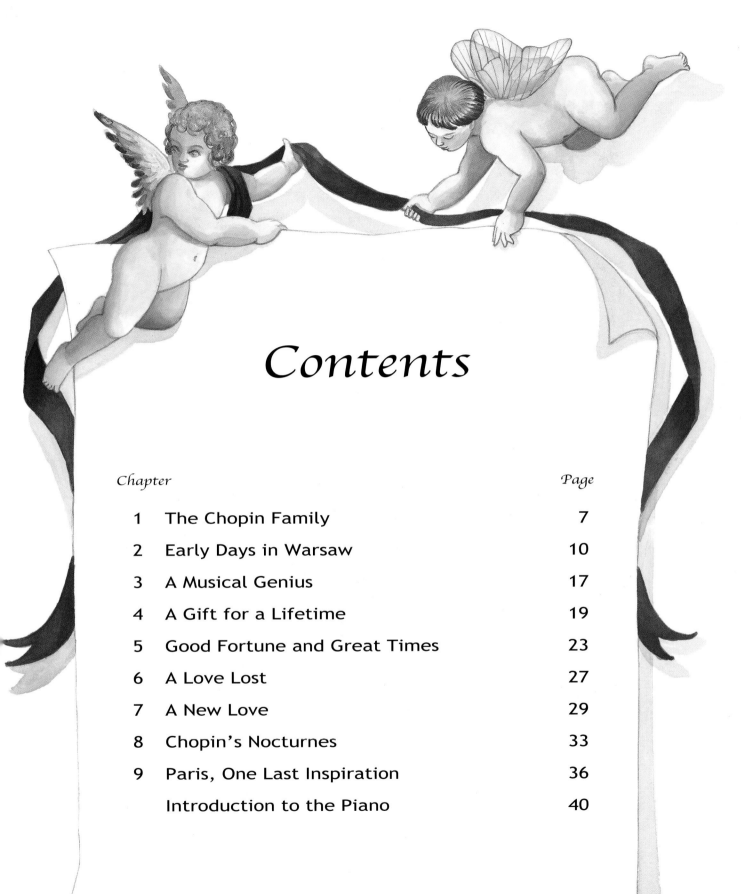

Contents

Żelazowa
Wola

Chapter 1
The Chopin Family

Frederic Chopin (pronounced SHOH-pan) was born on February 22, 1810, in the town of Zelazowa Wola, Poland. At that time, Frederic's father, Nicholas, and his mother, Justyna, lived at the home of Count Skarbek. His parents had met there. His mother was a distant relative of the Count, and his father worked as a French teacher for the Count's children.

Nicholas and Justyna married and had a baby girl they named Ludwika. Three years later, when Frederic was born, his family had no way of knowing that he would become a world-famous pianist and composer. Two more girls, Izabela and Emilia, were born to complete the family.

Chapter 2
Early Days in Warsaw

In 1815, when Chopin was five years old, his father moved the family to Warsaw, the capital of Poland. Chopin's father set up a private school there to teach French. In Chopin's day, children of wealthy families were taught French. The school developed a good reputation.

Chopin's mother taught music at the school, assisted by a young man named Mr. Zywny. Although Frederic was too young to take music lessons, he would sit quietly and listen as his mother and Mr. Zywny taught the students.

Mr. Zywny was impressed by Frederic's interest in music so he offered to teach him to play the piano. Frederic's extraordinary musical talents soon became apparent. He learned very quickly and was enthusiastic about practicing.

Chopin gave his first public performance at the age of seven, an impressive accomplishment for a young boy. When Frederic was eight, one of his piano scores was published—another

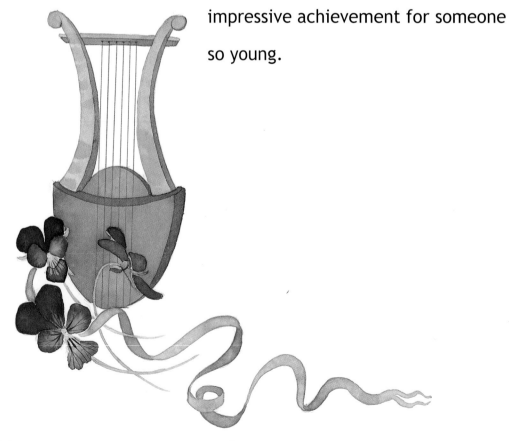

impressive achievement for someone so young.

Chopin's performance was so well-received that he was showered with kind words and gifts. His reputation spread as he continued to perform.

Although Chopin became famous quickly, he was said to have remained polite and quiet. As he grew older, he began playing in a local hotel in Berlin, Germany.

Chapter 3
A Musical Genius

In 1826, Chopin became a student at the Warsaw Conservatory. There, his work received great praise from his professors. One teacher marked the event of his graduation in 1829 by declaring Chopin a musical genius.

Chopin began traveling to other cities in countries outside of Poland. He usually traveled with his father or with friends.

In the summer of 1829, Chopin and his father visited Vienna, a cultural center of the time. Chopin met many of Vienna's most important citizens. He also went to concerts, literary readings, and art shows.

Chopin had the chance to perform in Vienna as well. His performances were well-received. Chopin became even more well-known.

Chapter 4
A Gift for a Lifetime

On his return trip to Warsaw, Chopin fell in love with a singer named Konstancja Gladkowska. Unfortunately, she did not return his love. He expressed his sadness through his music.

In 1830, at the age of 20, Chopin played his final concert in Poland. He then left Warsaw once again to visit other European cities. Before he left, his friends had a farewell party for him and gave him a silver goblet filled with Polish soil. This gift was meant to serve as a reminder of his homeland and of the contributions he had made to Poland.

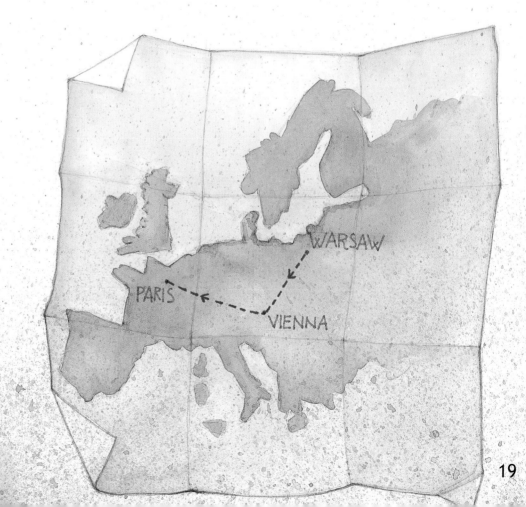

Chopin visited Vienna again in 1830 and then settled in Paris a year later. Chopin enjoyed living in the exciting city of Paris. He easily became friends with artists and musicians, including a man named Hector Berlioz, one of the most prominent musicians of the time.

Chopin had many opportunities to earn money by performing. Paris was an expensive city to live in, though. He often found it difficult to make ends meet.

Chapter 5
Good Fortune and Great Times

One day in Paris, Chopin's luck changed. While strolling through the streets, he met Prince Radziwill of Poland. The Prince invited Chopin to perform at his castle. Prince Radziwill was so impressed by Chopin and his music that he offered to help the composer earn money.

The Prince introduced Chopin to French nobility and to Polish nobles who had settled in France. Not only was Chopin a brilliant musician, but he was also considered handsome and charming. This made him very popular, and he organized concerts and taught piano lessons in the upper-class social circles.

Chopin traveled through Europe with other musicians. He attended performances of many talented composers, and their different musical styles helped to shape his own.

In 1835, Chopin traveled to the town of Karlsbad (today found in the Czech Republic) to join his family for a reunion. After spending time there, his family traveled back to Warsaw, and Chopin began his journey back to Paris.

Chapter 6
A Love Lost

On his way back to Paris, Chopin stopped in Dresden, Germany, for a short time. There, he visited the Wodzinski family, a Polish noble family. During his visit, he met the Wodzinski's daughter, Maria, and fell in love with her.

After he returned to Paris, he wrote Maria several love letters and composed many beautiful songs for her. Frederic and Maria were very much in love, but Maria's family did not allow the couple to marry because Chopin was not a wealthy noble. Once again, Chopin was disappointed in love.

Chapter 7
A New Love

Not long afterwards, Chopin met a woman named Aurore Dudevant at a ball. She was a well-known writer who went by the name of George Sand. Often, Aurore invited artists and composers to her country home in Nohant. When Chopin came to visit, they instantly fell in love.

Frederic and Aurore never married, but they spent several years together. In the winter of 1838, Frederic sailed with Aurore and her children to the Spanish island of Majorca. There, they enjoyed the warm sunshine and mild weather.

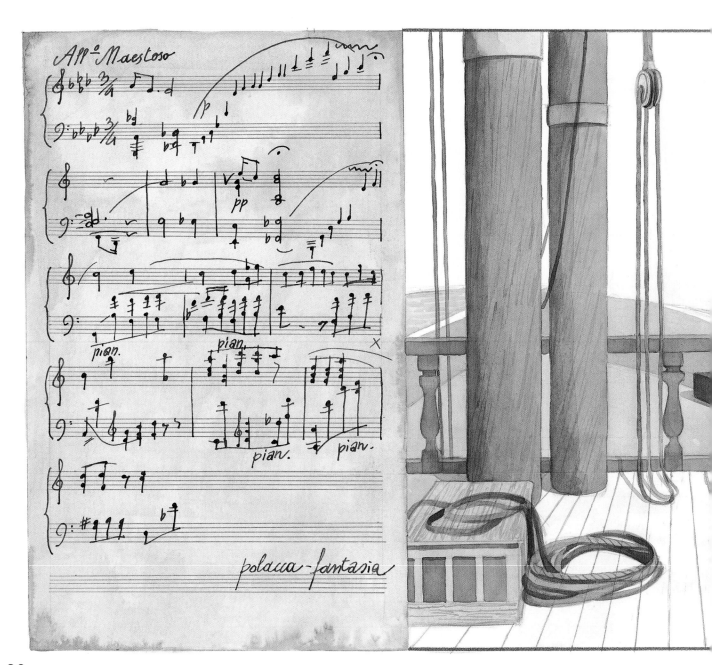

Soon the sunny weather gave way to strong winds and pouring rain. Chopin, who was often sick, developed a terrible disease called tuberculosis. He and Aurore stayed in Majorca for a few months, but Chopin's illness only got worse. Finally, they decided to go back to France.

Chapter 8
Chopin's Nocturnes

Chopin lived in Paris, but he spent his summers in Aurore's country home in Nohant. They lived there in luxury, and often shared their home with people from all over the world. Their eight years together, though, was filled with both happiness and conflict. The two separated in the summer of 1847.

Even though Chopin was still seriously ill, he continued to compose. His work reflected the different events in his life and his great sensitivity. Several of his pieces were called *nocturnes*, which are works of art about nighttime. These soft and romantic musical pieces bring to mind images of moonlit nights.

During the last years of his life, Chopin continued to suffer from illness. He did not have the strength to perform in public very often. He took a trip to England with his friend, Jane Stirling, one of his students and admirers. She helped Chopin earn money by arranging for him to play some concerts in private homes. He was paid very well for these concerts.

Toward the end of 1848, Chopin performed in London. It was his final public performance.

Chapter 9
Paris, One Last Inspiration

*A*fter he returned to Paris, Chopin lived in a house near the center of the city. From his window, he had a magnificent view. The city both comforted and inspired him.

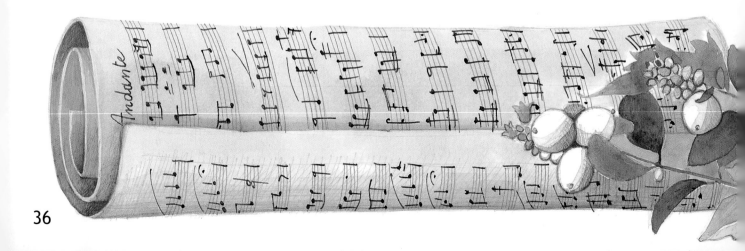

Chopin's health continued to worsen. When his eldest sister heard about his condition, she came to Paris to care for him.

Chopin passed away on October 17, 1849, at the age of 39. The Polish soil that his friends had given him so long ago was sprinkled on his coffin. He was laid to rest in Père La Chaise Cemetery in Paris, where, even today, admirers lay flowers on his grave.

Chopin composed over 200 works for the piano. This musical instrument was invented in 1709 by an Italian man named Bartolomeo Cristofori. The invention was hailed as an improvement over the harpsichord, because the player could control the loudness and length of the sound.

No single instrument can produce as wide a range of sounds as the piano. It is a keyboard instrument, usually with 88 keys. The piano commonly has two pedals to adjust the sound. When the performer touches the keys, felt-covered hammers strike the steel wire strings inside the body of the instrument. This produces the sounds.

Pianos vary in size and model. Today, there are two basic types—grand pianos (shown right), that are available in different sizes, and upright pianos which have vertical body frames. Grand pianos are quite large and are used mainly by concert pianists.

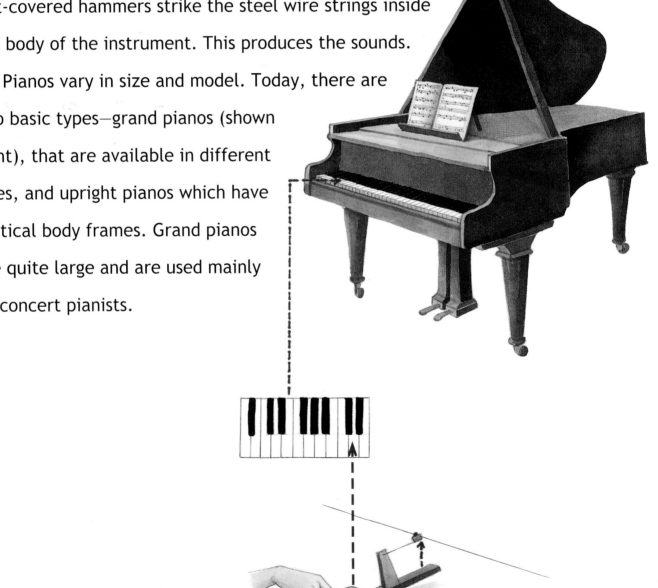